WE TRAVEL.
JOIN US IN OUR
JOURNEYS

http://kunzum.com

http://slideshare.net/kunzum

http://facebook.com/kunzum

http://vimeo.com/kunzum

@kunzum #wetravel

http://youtube.com/kunzum

CONTACT US
Kunzum Travel Café, T-49, GF, Hauz Khas Village
New Delhi 110 016, India
mail@kunzum.com | +91.99100 44476 | +91.9650 702 777

phew!

finally a place for travellers to meet.
in the real world - not on social media.

to simply bum around. exchange travel stories. make travel plans.

photographic art. even write books.

over coffee and cookies. and free wi-fi. only at the

kunzum
Travel Cafe

AUTHOR SPEAK

It has taken over 10,000 kilometers of driving (all by self) over a period of 14 months on Indian highways to collect all the road signs and advertisements in this book. I would call this the best phase of my professional life, giving me an opportunity to explore the northern part of India in a never before manner.

My travels took me to the Indian Himalayan regions of Ladakh, Himachal Pradesh and Uttarakhand (formerly Uttaranchal) for the purpose; I also took a few shots in New Delhi. I hope this collection provides enough fodder for your funny bone.

If you have traveled by road in the Indian Himalayas, many of these signs may give you a sense of déjà vu. Some of you may have even seen all of these, and more. But I still hope you enjoy these, and do so every time you open the book. Likewise for those around you.

I actually wanted to call this book Horn Please; you will find this expression all over the country and printed on almost every commercial vehicle you can see. But ubiquity meant others beat me to the title: there is already one by the same name in the market, and I am aware of at least two more in the pipeline. Thus my 'horn' went 'Peep Peep' instead.

If you come across signs like these in India, or anywhere else in the world, I would love to have you share those with me.

Isn't travel beautiful? And amusing too at times?

This edition first published 2008 by Kunzum,
the travel imprint of TCP Media Pvt. Ltd.

All Text and Photographs Copyright © 2008 by Ajay Jain

Designed by Dinesh Bisht
Edited by Nimish Dubey

Peep Peep Don't Sleep
by Ajay Jain - 1st edition

ISBN 978-81-906007-2-9

For ordering and other information write to:
mail@kunzum.com

Printed in India

CONTENTS

Near Kargil when going from <<
Alchi in Ladakh

HIMANK

YOU MAY NOT BE
SUPERSTITIOUS BUT
BELIEVE IN TRAFFIC SIGNS.

55 RCC   16 TF

PEEP PEEP
DONT
SLEEP

'You may not be superstitious, but believe in traffic signs.'

These are not my words, but those of a road sign on the way to Kargil from Leh in the Indian Himalayan region of Ladakh. You may as well agree with these because, as another one will tell you, 'Road Signs, They are the Signs of Life.' Driving on Indian highways can actually be a matter of life and death if one is not careful. After all, wouldn't you rather be 'Mr. Late' than 'Late Mr.' asks another one near Abbot Mount in the state of Uttarakhand.

Road Signs all over the world usually come up to ensure safe and smooth journeys for all travellers. It is no different on Indian highways. In their enthusiasm for public good, the state departments responsible for these seem to have gone many steps ahead. Someone told them about laughter being the best medicine, and they promptly put up amusing signs like 'Peep Peep Don't Sleep.' Puzzles and quizzes help keep the mind sharp, and they came up with brain twisters like 'Cution. Short cut may cut shorts.' To tease your imagination and keep you excited, they have a message 'I am Curveceous, Be Slow.'

HIMANK

ROAD SIGNS THEY ARE
SIGNS OF LIFE

753 TF   359 RMP   54 RCC

Extending a helping hand to Alcoholics Anonymous, they will tell you 'Whisky is Risky, Rum is Bomb.' In the interest of harmonious family ties, their advice goes, 'If you are married divorce your speed.' And just because you may be on roads at altitudes where aircrafts fly, you are reminded you are behind the wheel of a car with a SOS message of 'It is not a Runway, It is just a Hillway.' They have to play Big Daddy too with words of wisdom like 'Know Aids, No Aids' and 'When you are good to others, you are best to yourself.'

While many government entities may be competing (unofficially of course) to come up with the most witty, funny, strange, nonsensical and 'educative' messages, walking away with the honours are the Border Roads Organisation responsible for construction and maintenance of all roads in regions bordering countries like Pakistan, China, 'Tibet,' Nepal and Bhutan. When I travel with friends on these roads, we joke about who comes up with these signs. Do they have a secret government manual? Are these conjured up by the officers themselves over their evening quota of rum? Or outsourced to their housewives and girlfriends to help them overcome the boredom of being in remote locations or not being with them at all when they are posted in non-family stations?

Proud as they are of their efforts, they have erected signs patting themselves on the back. 'Sky is the limit, We take you there' and 'BRO's Blood Group is Zeal and Enthusiasm' are just some of the compliments you will get to read as you drive around.

Not that the private sector is too far behind. Storefronts, restaurants and hotels keep you entertained in good measure too. Advertisements amuse and will tickle your curiosity no end. All in all, keep your eyes

A few hours from Sarchu on
the way to Leh in Ladakh <<

roving, periscopic style, and you might find these signs as entertaining as the trip itself.

'If you want happiness for a lifetime, learn to love what you do.' The BRO seem to be loving the creative part of the job of building roads. And keeping travellers entertained even when they are bumping over rocky and pot-holed roads clearly looks a part of their job description. Who knows, these signs might even qualify for outdoor advertising awards some day.

The journey has started; 'Smile Please.' If you enjoy it, then let the whole world know by blowing your 'Horn Please.'

From Vijaypur to Munsiyari in <<
eastern Uttarakhand

WATCH THOSE CURVES

Curves: What kind of images does this word conjure up in your mind?

If you ask the Border Roads Organisation, they would talk of the seductive ways of the roads they build. Their roads are 'curveceous,' and they would advise you to 'drive your vehicle like playing a harp' on these. If you want to make progress, make sure you are 'mild on the curves;' you can also announce your intent and presence by 'honking' your 'horn' on these 'curves.'

A slight piece of warning though: 'Be soft on cauvers' (I think they meant curves) for 'speed thrills but kills.' Just like love, speed too can be a two-edged sword.

And here's a cryptic one for you to solve: 'Be short on curvs.' If you can crack this, you will be rewarded with the ability to understand women. Employees of BRO may not participate in this contest.

IS THE ROAD TRYING TO BE SEDUCTIVE HERE?

Near Leh on the way from Manali in Ladakh <<

On the outskirts of Leh in Ladakh <<

IN OTHER WORDS, YOU SHOULD KNOW
YOUR LIMITS

YOU ARE NOT GOING TO ATTRACT THE
ATTENTION OF THE 'CURVECEOUS' ONE TILL
YOU MAKE SOME NOISE.

From Manali to Rohtang Pass in <<
Himachal Pradesh

From Manali to Rohtang Pass in Himachal Pradesh <<

THESE MAY NOT BE AS DELICATE AS THEY SOUND

SLOW AND STEADY WINS THE RACE

From Abbot Mount to Patal Bhuvaneswar in the <<
eastern part of Uttarakhand

From Rohtang Pass to Jispa in <<
Himachal Pradesh

SOMEONE WANTS TO BE SERENADED HERE

THE NERVES NEED NOT FEEL RUFFLED IF YOU
ARE SLOW ON THESE CURVES

Near Kargil from Batalik in Ladakh <<

Near Bageshwar in the Kumaon <<
region of Uttarakhand

THEY EVEN SHORTENED THE SPELLING OF 'CURVES' TO SHOW THEY MEAN BUSINESS

HEED THIS ADVICE TO SAVE YOU FROM GOING
OVER THE BEND

From Abbot Mount to Patal Bhuvaneswar in the <<
eastern part of Uttarakhand

From Abbot Mount to Patal Bhuvaneswar in <<
the eastern part of Uttarakhand

THEY REALLY DON'T MEAN THERE IS A 'BAND' PLAYING A SLOW BEAT AROUND THE CORNER, DO THEY?

AFTER DRINKING
WHISKY
DRIVING IS RISKY

38 BRTF   70 RCC

THE
RIGHT
SPIRITS

The roads can be dangerous enough, and you certainly don't want to add to the risks by making a 'fatal cock-tail' of 'driving and drinking.' Liquor is, after all, one of the 'enemies of the road,' others being 'overload and speed.'

So, what is powering your driving? Hope it is not 'rum power' for, you must surely know, 'rum is bomb' just as 'whisky is risky.' Stick to the recommended gas for your wheels.

While on the subject of spirits, maybe someone should put up signs about the other 'high inducing' substances available in abundance, albeit discreetly, in places like Manali and Dharamsala. Judging by the way some of the local drivers drive, it seems they are packed with this potent stuff. But why fault them? After all, they have only been told that 'after drinking whisky, driving is risky.' There is no mention of anything else causing danger.

For the benefit of all those who tend to take to the wheel in a state of 'spirited happiness,' someone should perhaps establish a 'Drivers Anonymous.' Let us raise a toast to this.

THAT'S SOME HORSE SENSE BEING TALKED
ABOUT HERE

In the Nubra Valley in Ladakh <<

From Leh to Kargil via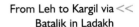
Batalik in Ladakh

SO WHAT ARE VODKA, WINE AND TEQUILA?

NEVER DRINK AND DRIVE
IN THE HILLS
IT WILL COST DEARER
TO YOUR LIVES

38 BRTF   70 RCC

IT IS EVIDENTLY FINE TO DRINK IN THE PLAINS!!

Near Sarchu on the border of Himachal <<
Pradesh and Ladakh

Near Siachen Glacier in Ladakh <<

WHAT IS THE HYPHEN IN 'COCK-TAIL' SUPPOSED TO MEAN?

On the road to Siachen Glacier in Nubra <<
Valley in Ladakh

DRINK AND DRIVE, YO WON'T SURVIVE

YO! YOU CAN BET ON THIS ONE TO BE TRUE!!

A couple of hours before Leh when going <<
from Manali in Ladakh

AT LEAST YOU CANNOT PUT ALL THE BLAME
ON THE DRINKING

DIESEL AND PETROL WILL DO

In the Nubra Valley in Ladakh <<

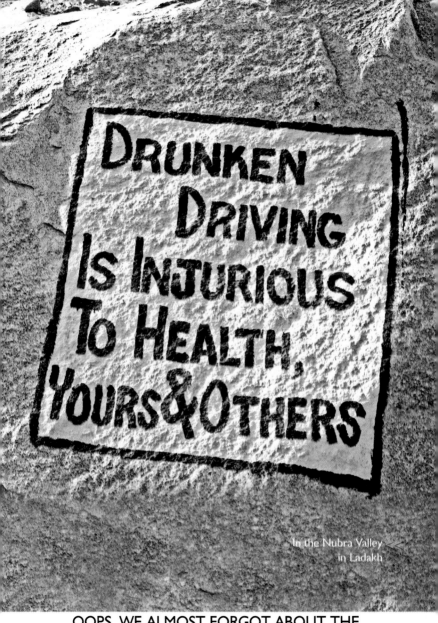

In the Nubra Valley
in Ladakh

OOPS, WE ALMOST FORGOT ABOUT THE
OTHERS ON THE ROAD!!

EVEN IF YOU ARE NOT GOING TO A PARTY,
SHOULD YOU BE DRIVING DIRTY?

At Sarchu on the road to Leh in Ladakh <<

Darling,
De not nag me, as I am driving.
Instead turn your head,
And enjoy the nature charming

SM

For all forest related information please contact :- Divisional Forest Officer
Mussoorie Forest Division
BROOKLAND ESTATE, MUSSOORIE.
PHONE: 0135-2652330

From Dehradun to Mussoorie, the capital of <<
the state of Uttarakhand

THE NEAR
AND
DEAR ONES

Want to tell your partner she is being a 'nag', and should 'turn her head to enjoy the nature charming while you are driving' but lack the nerve to do so? Relax, help is at hand from the ever-caring road builders; they have put up these messages on your behalf.

And for both the partners too. So while the passenger is told 'don't gossip, let him drive,' the driver (who, for some reason, is always supposed to be male) is reminded about love being conditional when she says, 'Darling I like you but not so fast.' And to drive home the message more firmly, she adds, 'If you love me, divorce speed.' Pay heed here unless you want a separation from more than just speed.

Practice 'safety' and your family will have 'safe tea' waiting for you at home. (Too bad if you have a preference for coffee!) And then go for a walk around the house so you may 'love the neighbour' which is not advised you do 'while driving.'

If your eyes start drooping, grab a can of Red Bull because 'if you sleep your family will weep.' Anyone carrying Kleenex tissues here?

Around Leh in Ladakh

SHE IS TALKING ABOUT THE SPEED OF THE
CAR, WE ARE SURE!

Near Dharamsala in <<
Himachal Pradesh

MICHAEL SCHUMACHER WOULD HAVE HAD
NO CHANCE WITH HER!!

NOW HERE'S A STERN ONE FOR THE LADY...BUT
DO ONLY LADIES GOSSIP?

Near Leh when coming from Nubra <<
Valley in Ladakh

SOMEONE IS FINALLY GETTING THE MESSAGE

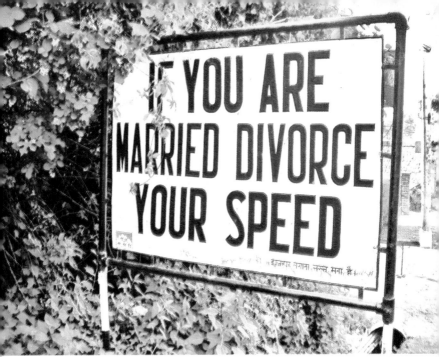

SINGLES DO HAVE MORE FUN, INCLUDING BEING
ALLOWED TO LIVE LIFE IN THE FAST LANE

Near Dharamsala in <<
Himachal Pradesh

YOUR FAMILY WAITS FOR YOU. NOT FOR THE NEWS OF YOUR ACCIDENT

55 RCC

16 TF

Near Kargil in Ladakh <<

YOU DON'T WANT TO BE THE BREAKING NEWS
YOURSELF FOR THE WRONG REASONS, DO YOU?

NOW, THAT SHOULD BE AN INCENTIVE

Between Jispa and Sarchu on <<
way to Ladakh

From Leh to Alchi in Ladakh <<

AND THEN YOU WILL ALSO NOT GET ANY TEA

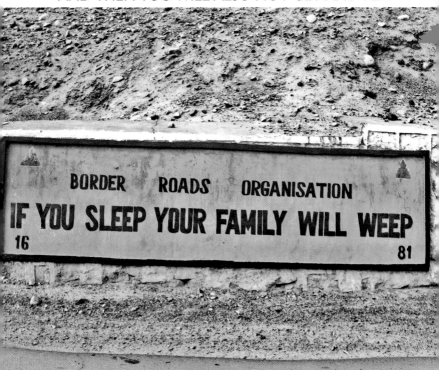

In the Nubra Valley in Ladakh <<

WHAT WILL THE WIFE THINK OF THIS?

BORDER ROADS
ORGANISATION

FAST·WON'T LAST

65RCC   21TF

Near Abbot Mount in <<
eastern Uttarakhand

(NOT) IN THE FAST LANE

The Himalayas can do things to the adrenalin; the sights and the air just seem to keep pumping more of it. And when you are on these sky hugging roads, mostly empty bar a few passing vehicles, it is not difficult to develop delusions of being behind the wheels of a F1 car or in the cockpit of a jet plane.

The road builders know we all have these 'super-hero' instincts within us and thus warn us to 'Drive, Don't Fly.' Remember, they add, you are on a 'hillway,' not a 'runway;' those who 'drive slow, live long' and any-ways 'fast won't last.'

Instead, try slow travel to capture the essence of places you visit. After all, 'mountains are a pleasure only if you travel with leisure.' Do you know what they say when you don't heed such advice? 'Worse it comes with no warning, prevent it by careful driving.' Admirable sentiments, once you can untangle the words.

In the meantime, ease up on the accelerator.

Between Batalik and
Kargil in Ladakh

IT IS ALSO COMMON SENSE, RIGHT?

From Abbot Mount to Patal Bhuvaneswar in <<
the eastern part of Uttarakhand

THIS SEEMS TO HAVE TYPOS IN MORE WAYS THAN ONE

From Kargil to Leh <<
in Ladakh

YOU DON'T WANT THAT SILLY LOOK ON YOUR
FACE SHOULD THINGS GO WRONG!

ARE THEY ASKING A BAND TO BLOW ITS HORN, OR TELLING YOU TO BLOW YOUR HORN PLEASE ON THE BEND? PERHAPS IT DEPENDS ON THE SPEED OF YOUR 'CHEAK!'

Top Line: Please Drive Slow Keep Left (India follows the British system of road driving)

Hindi Translation: Follow traffic rules, and reach your destination safe. Blow your horn.

Second English Line: Please Speed Your Cheak

Third English Line: Please Band Horn Bajao

('Horn Bajao' means 'Blow Your Horn')

Munsiyari in eastern part of Uttarakhand <<

AND PLAY SOME ENTERTAINING MUSIC
TO ADD TO THE MOOD

From Kargil to Leh in Ladakh <<

In the Nubra Valley in Ladakh

DRIVE, DON'T FLY

YOU CAN IF YOU WANT TO THOUGH; THE HIGH ROADS OF THE HIMALAYAS ARE THE PERFECT TAKE OFF - IF YOUR CAR CAN PARAGLIDE THAT IS!

NO JUMBO JETS HERE PLEASE

On the Manali Rohtang Pass road, <<
Himachal Pradesh

From Alchi to Kargil <<
in Ladakh

Near Bhimtal, when coming from <<
Nainital in Uttarakhand

AND NO FORMULA ONE EITHER ON THESE ROADS

IT IS NOT
RALLY OR RACE
YOU CAN DRIVE
WITH GRACE.

38 ERTF   70 RCC

YOU CAN ALWAYS PARTICIPATE IN THE
HIMALAYAN CAR RALLY IF ADVENTURE IS WHAT
YOU SEEK

Near Jispa when coming from Leh <<
in Himachal Pradesh

Near the Siachen Glacier in Ladakh <<

HE HAS SPOKEN, YOU BETTER LISTEN!

BORDER ROADS
ORGANISATION
FAST DRIVING
LAST DRIVING
761   65

DO YOU WANT THIS DRIVE TO BE YOUR
SWANSONG?

Near Abbot Mount in <<
eastern Uttarakhand

Between Manali and Rohtang <<
Pass in Himachal Pradesh

Near the Lamayuru Monastery <<
in Ladakh

A SPEEDING DRIVER GATHERS NO YEARS

On way to Rohtang Pass << from Manali in Himachal Pradesh

MOUNTAINS ARE A PLEASURE ONLY IF YOU DRIVE WITH LEISURE

BRO
MOUNTAIN ARE PLEASURE ONLY IF YOU DRIVE WITH LEISURE
38 TF   DEEPAK   70 RCC

SHOP NO
88

SLOW TRAVEL IS IN

On way to Goriganga River Bed from <<
Munsiyari in eastern part of Uttarakhand

DOES THIS MEAN 'SAFTEY LIES IN BEING FAST' OR
'SAFETY FIRST'? WE ARE SCRATCHING OUR HEADS!

NO OVER TAKING,
NO ACCIDENTS

In the Nubra Valley
in Ladakh

EVEN IF YOU ARE STUCK BEHIND A
BULLOCK CART?

Near Upshi when going from Leh to <<
Manali in Ladakh

WORSE IT COMES WITH

NO WARNING PREVENT

IT BY CAREFUL DRIVING

JULE

753TF   IIIRCC

A TRULY MYSTICAL MESSAGE - THIS ONE IS FOR
YOU TO INTERPRET.
'Jule' is a welcome or God Bless greeting in Ladhaki

BORDER ROADS ORGANISATION

BE MR LATE
BETTER THAN LATE MR

DRIVE

Near Abbot Mount in eastern <<
Uttarakhand

DIE ANOTHER DAY

For those who have not been taking the road 'safty' messages seriously so far, time for some tough talking: we are all destined to keep our appointment with the 'undertaker', but why rush it? After all, 'speed thrills but kills' too.

And 'short cuts' can not only 'cut short your life' but your 'shorts' too. If the latter does not make sense, it is probably a part of the job description of the copywriter of this message to make the riddle do to you what curiosity did to the cat. But a 'cat has nine lives but not one who drives.' Can you really afford to gamble away the one life you have?

And get yourself a good timekeeper too while you are at it. With warnings like, 'It is better to be 15 minutes late in the world than be 15 minutes early in the next' you don't want to lose out like the rally drivers who are docked points for using more time, and less as well, than stipulated for a given leg.

In the meantime, decide where you want to book a passage to: 'Heaven, Hell or Mother Earth.'

WHO SHOULD FEAR THE UNDERTAKER? THE
'OVERTAKER' OR THE 'OVERTAKEN'?

On the road to Leh from <<
Manali in Ladakh

On the road to Leh from <<
Manali in Ladakh

NEED TO DEVELOP SCENARIOS AT 60, 70
AND 80 TOO?

BODER ROADS ORGANISATION

OVERSPEED IS A KNIFE
THAT CUTE A LIFE

753BRTF   51RCC

Around Leh town in Ladakh <<

WHAT CAN BE SO CUTE ABOUT THIS?

From Manali to Rohtang Pass <<
in Himachal Pradesh

WOULD DRIVING SLOW BE A DISAGREEMENT?
ONE WONDERS...

CUTION .
SHORT CUTS
MAY CUT SHORTS

OOPS…THE REVELATIONS COULD BE
EMBARRASSING!!

From Patal Bhuvaneswar to Vijaypur in <<
eastern Uttarakhand

From Abbot Mount to Patal <<
Bhuvaneswar in the eastern part
of Uttarakhand

THIS MAKES MORE SENSE DESPITE THE
TYPOS...WHY CUT ANYONE'S SHORTS?

YOU COULD DIE TRYING TO INTERPRET THIS

Near Kargil in Ladakh <<

THROUGH THE WINDSCREEN ON A RAINY
EVENING: WHO IS KEEPING TIME HERE?

IT IS BETTER TO BE 15 MINUTES
LATE IN THE WORLD THAN BE 15 MINUTES
EARLY IN THE NEXT.

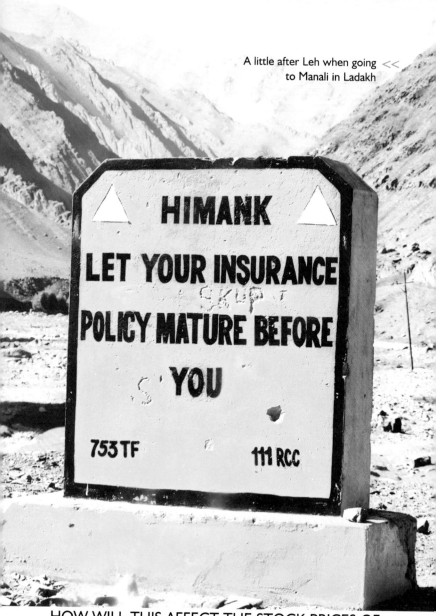

A little after Leh when going << to Manali in Ladakh

HIMANK

LET YOUR INSURANCE

POLICY MATURE BEFORE

YOU

753 TF   111 RCC

HOW WILL THIS AFFECT THE STOCK PRICES OF INSURANCE COMPANIES?

In the Nubra Valley
in Ladakh

YOU WILL ALSO MISS OUT ON YOUR TICKET TO
NIRVANA
Reads: Drive Like Hell And You Will Be There

NOW YOU ARE BEING PROMISED HEAVEN; WHY
CAN'T SOMEONE MAKE UP THEIR MIND?

Near Upshi when going from Leh <<
to Manali in Ladakh

DID NOT KNOW THERE WAS A MENU TO CHOOSE
FROM; YOU ARE BEING SPOILT FOR CHOICE HERE.

Near Siachen Glacier <<
in Ladakh

SAVE THE ROAD? FROM WHOM?

PERHAPS THE YETI LIKES TAKING A 'SHOT'
AT RASH DRIVERS!!

SPEEDING DRIVERS - VULTURES AND
UNDERTAKERS LOVE 'EM

Near the Siachen Glacier <<
in Ladakh

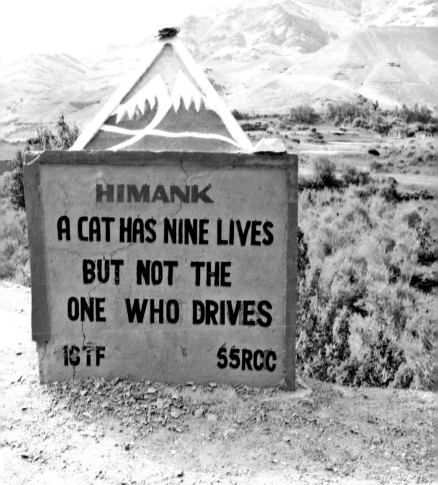

A few hours from Kargil when ≪
headed to Leh in Ladakh

HIMANK

A CAT HAS NINE LIVES
BUT NOT THE
ONE WHO DRIVES

16TF   55RCC

UNLESS YOU BELIEVE IN REINCARNATION

GENERAL RESERVE ENGINEER FORCE

NOT WITCHCRAFT
BUT WATCH CRAFT
THAT SAVES.

55 RCC   16 TF

On the road from Alchi to <<
Kargil in Ladakh

BETTER
SAFE THAN
SORRY

Remember the three women with the cauldron conjuring up magic potions, but could still not save either Macbeth or the king? If you are not careful, no amount of 'witchcraft' will be able to save you either; you will need to rely on 'watchcraft' only.

This includes being 'ready when others make mistakes' and not being 'rash' lest you 'end in crash.' Don't forget to 'cheak your brakes' too; if you don't 'mind your brakes' it will 'break your mind.' You may have heard of the AA (Automobile Association); there is now the AAA: 'Aleart Avoid Accident.'

And don't 'daydream;' you have a journey to complete. Safely, for rescue missions may not always be at hand. The Border Roads Organisation does challenge drivers to 'drive fast and test our recovery.' Does this mean they will be super fast or super slow? Do you really want to find out?

I AM AWAKE; ONLY MY EYES ARE CLOSED.

From Sarchu to Leh in Ladakh <<

A little after Kargil on the <<
road to Leh in Ladakh

BORDER ROADS ORGANISATION

DRIVING AND DAY DREAMING DO NOT GO TOGETHER

16   55

YES, YOU COULD BE SLEEPING EVEN WITH
YOUR EYES OPEN

ARE YOU AN A-GRADER?

At the Birthi Falls on the way to <<
Munsiyari in eastern Uttarakhand

On the road from Alchi to <<
Kargil in Ladakh

NO, IT HAS NOTHING TO DO WITH TURNING
THE OTHER CHEEK

BORDR ROADS ORGANISATION

MIND YOUR BRAKES
OR BREAK YOUR MIND.

55 RCC   16 TF

On the road from Alchi to
Kargil in Ladakh

THE CHOICE IS YOURS

Near Upshi on the route from
Leh to Manali in Ladakh

HIMANK
DRIVING FASTER
CAN
CAUSE DISASTER
BRO
753TF   IIIRCC

LORD BYRON COULD NOT HAVE
RHYMED IT BETTER

HOPEFULLY, THEY WON'T BE 'SLOW' IN
REACHING YOU

Near Pang on the Leh - Manali <<
route in Ladakh

On the road from Kargil to <<
Leh in Ladakh

UNLESS A BUMPER-TO-BUMPER CRASH IS YOUR IDEA OF FUN

ARE YOU READY WHEN OTHERS MAKE MISTAKES, BE A DEFENSIVE DRIVER

55 RCC

16 TF

YOU CANNOT BE HELD RESPONSIBLE FOR
EVERYTHING THAT HAPPENS, CAN YOU?

Near Kargil when coming from <<
Leh in Ladakh

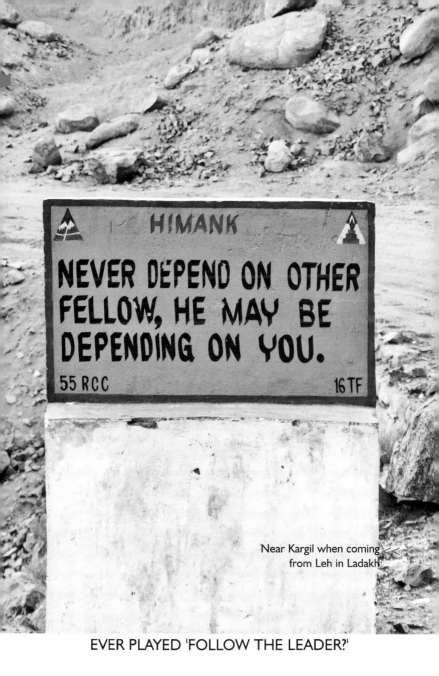

EVER PLAYED 'FOLLOW THE LEADER?'

NO ONE HAS A POETIC LICENCE TO
DRIVE RASHLY

Near Kargil when coming from <<
Leh in Ladakh

Going from Manali to Rohtang Pass <<
in Himachal Pradesh

ARE YOU WEARING A LIFE JACKET?

BORDER ROADS ORGANISATION
HIMANK

ACCIDENT BEGINS WHERE ALERTNESS ENDS.

55 RCC

16 TF

Near Kargil in Ladakh <<

ZEN AND THE ART OF SURVIVAL

Call these the ABCs of safe driving; follow these and you will earn yourself the title of the 'wise man who drives safely.'

All you need to do is adopt a few good practices - 'start early' and 'drive slowly' are just two of the simple ones. Do 'keep your cool' when driving and 'take it easy' no matter what or who is testing your patience.

Also remember 'accident begins where alertness ends' but the 'cautious seldom err.' And keep reminding yourself, 'Safety is checking before moving.'

One last bit of advice: 'Follow the road sign boards.' Even when they are funny or incomprehensible.

TRICKS OF SURVIVAL ON HILLS ROADS

START EARLY

DRIVE SLOWLY

REACH SAFELY

38 BRTF   370 RCC

YOU JUST ATTENDED THE BEGINNER'S CLASS!

Going from Rohtang Pass to Jispa <<
on the road to Ladakh

BORDER ROADS ORGANISATION

FOR YOUR SAFETY ONLY

1. DRIVE SLOW IN ALL THE BRIDGES
2. FOLLOW THE ROAD SIGN BOARDS
3. GIVE PASSACE TO LIGHT VEHICLES
4. COOPERATE WITH TCP

753TF   491RMP   54RCC

In the ≪
Nubra
Valley in
Ladakh

...MASTERS

MOVING ON TO ADVANCED LESSONS
TCP stands for 'Traffic Check Post' manned by the Army

EXCEPT WHEN SPELLING 'THE'
Himank is the division of the Border Roads
Organisation in Ladakh

In Nubra Valley on road to <<
Siachen Galcier in Ladakh

In Nubra Valley on road to Siachen <<
Galcier in Ladakh

TIME WAITS FOR EVERYONE HERE

STAND UNDER A WATERFALL; YOU WILL FIND
PLENTY IN THE MOUNTAINS

On the way to Alchi from <<
Leh in Ladakh

In Nubra Valley on road to <<
Siachen Galcier in Ladakh

WHAT ABOUT CHECKING AS YOU MOVE ALONG?

In Nubra Valley on road to <<
Siachen Galcier in Ladakh

THE SIGHTS DO GET ONE EXCITED, BUT DON'T
FORGET YOU ARE BEHIND A WHEEL

In Nubra Valley on road to <<
Siachen Galcier in Ladakh

AND WHO IS A WISE WOMAN?

COUNTER-ATTACK WITH SHOOTING STARS!!

From Manali to Rohtang Pass in <<
Himachal Pradesh

From Manali to Rohtang Pass in <<
Himachal Pradesh

AND DON'T GO CRASHING INTO ANY TREES

GENERAL RESERVE ENGINEER FORCE
HIMANK
DIVIDED ATTENTION
EQUALS MULTIPLIED
TROUBLES.

Near Batalik on way to Kargil <<
in Ladakh

THE
WISE MEN
SPEAKETH...

Do you miss your father when you travel? The road builders ensure you don't by providing you advice on how to lead your life, delivered daddy-style. So what if the 'child is the father of the nation;' your father is still your father.

Heard the famous words: I think therefore I am? The corollary to that now is, 'Without Geography you are nowhere.' It may thus be a good idea to carry an atlas with you at all times. And when it guides you to the 'land of lama,' make sure you are not a 'gama' there. Foxed? So is everyone else. Try being alpha or beta instead. Poor joke.

Stop looking around for help; 'divided attention' can lead to 'multiplied troubles.' Focus on reading these pages.

THE हिमांक

KNOW AIDS
NO AIDS

253 TF   111 RCC

BRO

THAT IS A SENSIBLE ONE TO START WITH

A little beyond Leh when going <<
to Manali in Ladakh

In Nubra Valley in Leh <<

HOW MUCH EFFORT WAS MADE WITH THE TYPOS ON THIS ONE?

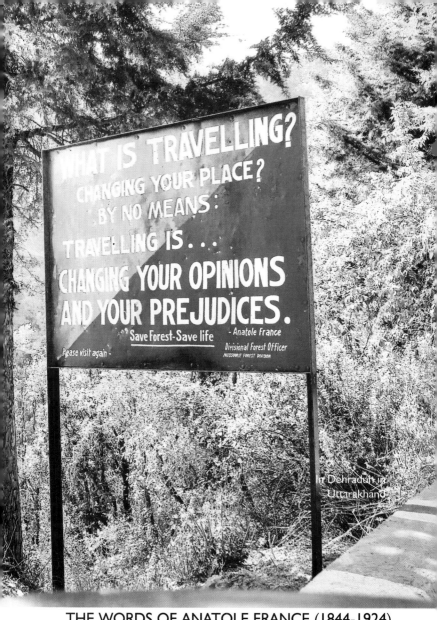

WHAT IS TRAVELLING?
CHANGING YOUR PLACE?
BY NO MEANS:

TRAVELLING IS . . . .

CHANGING YOUR OPINIONS
AND YOUR PREJUDICES.

Save Forest-Save life   — Anatole France

Please visit again —   Divisional Forest Officer
                                    MUSSOORIE FOREST DIVISION

In Dehradun in
Uttarakhand

THE WORDS OF ANATOLE FRANCE (1844-1924),
IMMORTALIZED BY THE FOREST DEPARTMENT IN
THE INDIAN HIMALAYAS

In Nubra Valley in Ladakh <<

NO MATTER HOW CONFIDENT YOU ARE OF HAVING DONE A GOOD JOB, THE BOSS WILL NEVER BE PLEASED

DO GOOD TO THE AUTHOR - BUY MORE COPIES
OF THIS BOOK

When going from Leh to <<
Kargil via Batalik

IS IT ALSO GOOD ROAD SENSE?

BORDER ROADS ORGANISATION

IF YOU WANT HAPPINESS
FOR A LIFE TIME LEARN
TO LOVE WHAT YOU DO

16TF   55RCC

FALL IN LOVE WITH DRIVING SAFE TOO

On the Kargil Leh route near <<
Lamayuru in Ladakh

In Nubra Valley in Ladakh <<

DON'T IMITATE. BE ORGINAL.

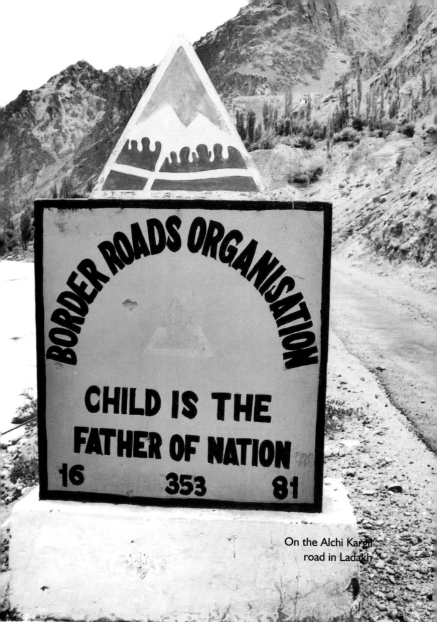

BORDER ROADS ORGANISATION

CHILD IS THE
FATHER OF NATION

16   353   81

On the Alchi Kargil road in Ladakh

THIS SOUNDS LIKE A COMPLICATED FAMILY TREE

NEED TO LEARN BUDDHIST TO INTERPRET
THIS ONE

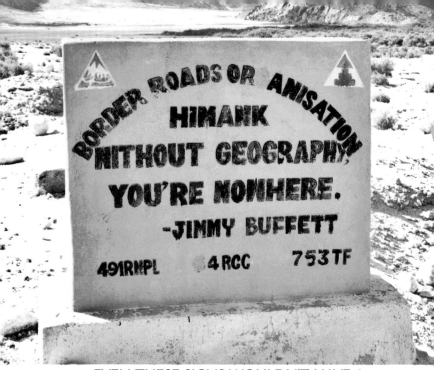

EVEN THESE SIGNS WOULDN'T HAVE A PLACE TO GO

In Nubra Valley in Ladakh <<

In Nubra Valley in Ladakh <<

IS IT SOMETHING ABOUT BEER AND FRIENDS HERE?

BUT WE LIVE IN COMPLEX TIMES?

In Nubra Valley in <<
Ladakh

From Nubra Valley to
Leh in Ladakh <<

TRAFIC JAM
YELLOW
TAPE
PARENT
CRYING.

EVEN SOCRATES WOULD HAVE BEEN
STUMPED BY THIS

BORDER ROADS ORGANISATION

HIMANK

A DEAD END
IS JUST A GOOD PLACE
TO TURN AROUND.
- NAOMI JUDD

491RMPL   54 RCC   753TF

SIACHIN TREAD MASTERS

In Nubra Valley in Ladakh

YOU COULD KEEP GOING AND SEE WHAT LIES
ON THE OTHER SIDE

On way from Alchi to
Kargil in Ladakh

LIFE CAN BE FULL OF SURPRISES

TRANSLATED, IT MEANS JUST KEEP SMILING

In the Nubra Valley on the road to Siachen <<
Glacier in Ladakh

From Kargil to Leh in Ladakh <<

WHO WILL CLEAR THE TYRE MARKS?

WHAT ABOUT SHARING LUNCH?
The last word reads as 'Others'

In the Nubra Valley in Ladakh <<

In the Nubra Valley in Ladakh <<

AFTER ALL, TOMORROW NEVER DIES

From Leh to Nubra <<
Valley in Ladakh

BLOWING
THEIR OWN
'HORN'

A pat on the back is always good for morale. And indulging in a bit of self-congratulations can be good too when others are not being very appreciative. The Border Roads Organisation would not disagree. After all, their 'blood group is zeal and enthusiasm.'

Are they deserving of such praise? Of course they are. For them, the 'sky is the limit' and they promise to 'take you there.' But before you rush to pack your bags check out another of their signs reading, 'BRO can construct roads anywhere except the sky.' This is confusing: Does one get a ride to the skies or not?

The lovelorn can also bank on the BRO for some solace; the latter claim to 'cut through the hills but joins the hearts.' Not only hearts, they also 'connect Ladakh to the best of the world.' Why are they connecting only to the 'best?' Has the 'rest' of the world earned their ire in some way?

That said, as the BRO is 'tips to toes in the service of the nation,' let us raise three quarters of a toast to them.

LET'S PRESENT 'HIMANK' WITH A DICTIONARY ON THEIR ANNUAL DAY

Himank is the division of the Border Roads Organisation in Ladakh

From Kargil to Leh <<
in Ladakh

In Nubra Valley on road to <<
Siachen Glacier in Ladakh

THE BRO (BORDER ROADS ORGANISATION) SHOULD LOOK BACK SOMETIMES, TO SPOT THE ROADS LEFT BROKEN

WAY TO GO…WHO NEEDS APOLLO
OR DISCOVERY?

From Leh to Nubra <<
Valley in Ladakh

In Nubra Valley on road to <<
Siachen Glacier in Ladakh

WHAT ABOUT THE PROMISE TO TAKE
US TO THE SKIES?

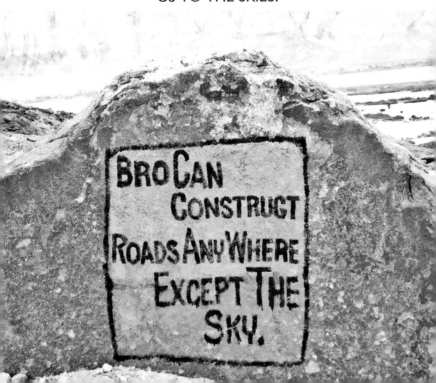

IF YOU WISH UP ON A STAR NO WONDER WHERE YOU ARE BORDER ROADS WILL TAKE YOU THERE

THEY ARE PROMISING THE MOON AGAIN. WILL
WE GET ROADS AMONGST THE 'TWINKLE
TWINKLE LITTLE STARS'?

In Nubra Valley on road to Siachen <<
Glacier in Ladakh

In Nubra Valley on road to <<
Siachen Glacier in Ladakh

GOOD NEWS FOR ALL PRESENT DAY ROMEOS WHOSE JULIETS LIVE ON THE OTHER SIDE OF HIGH MOUNTAIN PASSES

WHERE WAS BRO WHEN MY CAR WAS STRUGGLING OVER THE 'MOON-CRATERED' ROAD TO ZANSKAR?

Read as: Snow Clad Mountains, Scorching Deserts, Inaccessible Pockets, BRO is seen everywhere

In Nubra Valley on road to <<
Siachen Glacier in Ladakh

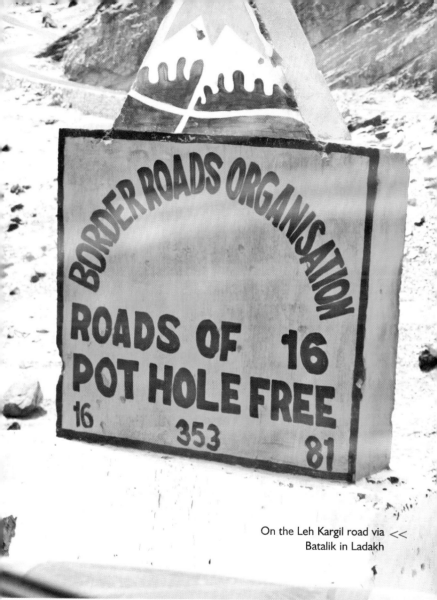

BORDER ROADS ORGANISATION

ROADS OF
POT HOLE FREE
16
16
353
81

On the Leh Kargil road via <<
Batalik in Ladakh

THE JURY IS OUT ON THIS ONE, AND THEIR CARS
ARE IN THE WORKSHOPS AFTER A DRIVE ON
SOME OF THE ROADS.

IT IS TOO LATE ON SOME OF THE ROADS

Near Leh when coming from <<
Nubra Valley in Ladakh

From Jispa to Sarchu in <<
Himachal Pradesh

IMPOSSIBLE WILL TAKE TIME
DIFFICULT WILL BE DONE
IMMEDIATELY
70 RCC   38 TF

REMEMBER THE TAG LINE OF A FAMOUS SHOE
BRAND THAT READS 'IMPOSSIBLE IS NOTHING?'

IMPOSSIBLE IS DONE
IMMEDIATELY MIRACLE
TAKES A LITTLE
TIME

THEY ARE GETTING BETTER. THEY CAN NOW DO
THE 'IMPOSSIBLE' AT ONCE.

In Nubra Valley on road to <<
Siachen Glacier in Ladakh

In Nubra Valley on road to Siachen <<
Glacier in Ladakh

NOW WE KNOW WHO TO CALL WHEN FEELING DOWN IN THE DUMPS AND NEEDING A TRANSFUSION

IS THAT A PROMISE?

In Nubra Valley on road to <<
Siachen Glacier in Ladakh

In Nubra Valley on road to <<
Siachen Glacier in Ladakh

ONLY TIPS TO TOES? WHAT ABOUT THE REST?

Near Alchi when headed to <<
Zanskar Valley in Ladakh

HIMANK PROJECT
BORDER ROADS MAKE
AWAY FOR YOUR
BRIGHT FUTURE
16 TF   81

ARE THEY 'MAKING A WAY' OR DOING 'AWAY'
WITH THE BRIGHT FUTURE?

From Rohtang Pass to Jispa in <<
Himachal Pradesh

AYE, AYE, SIR!!

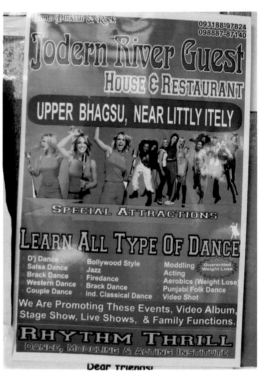

CAN YOU THINK OF ANY OTHER SINGLE LOCATION WHERE YOU CAN LEARN SO MANY FORMS OF INDIAN AND WESTERN DANCES (INCLUDING 'BRACK DANCE'), OR BECOME AN ACTOR OR A MODEL, WITH 'GUARANTEED WEIGHT LOSE' THROWN IN?

THE DHARAMSALA SCHOOL OF QUICK LEARNING

The Indian Himalayan state of Himachal Pradesh is referred to as Dev Bhoomi, or land of the Gods, by the locals. Their divine powers must really work enabling one to learn anything from the Hindi language to belly dancing to yoga and power meditation and more in a matter of days.

Welcome to the Dharamsala School of Quick Learning. Located in Himachal Pradesh, and home to the Dalai Lama, you can find enlightenment and knowledge being sold - fast food style - all over Dharamsala and the surrounding towns of Bhagsunag, Dharamkot and Mcleodganj.

If you are a woman, this may be your opportunity to 'unveil your feminine mystery with Monika' as her belly dancing classes are more than just that. The 'classes combine chakra energy work and meditation to create a unique and inspiring Shakti experience.' If this is still not enough, know more about the 'seven main energy centers' when you learn Reiki at the Buddha Hall. And for total 'revitalization of mind, body and spirits' learn power meditation at the Asho Institute; the '6 days course' comes with 'guranteed experiences.' Don't ask of what.

And if you wish to become familiar with the local Hindi language, 'Learn Hindi' and 'Feel the Voice of India' with Siddharth. Or go cultural. Learn classical Indian music in days and confound the Masters who otherwise spend years with their prodigies. Sitting in Dharamsala, you can learn the art of the times of the Muslim emperors who once ruled India besides modern and Tibetan Buddhist forms too. Or become a skilled craftsman in making silver jewelry in hours, not days.

What can be so impossible about picking up all these skills on the fast track? After all, isn't India the land of the mystic and the magical?

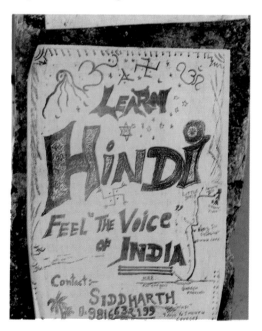

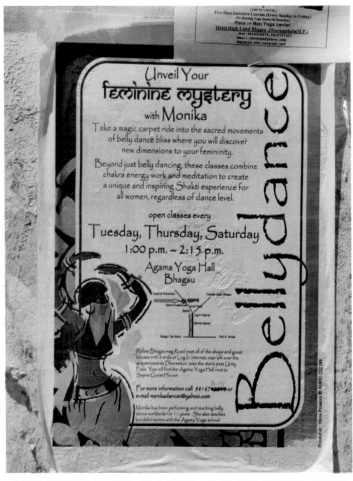

JUST BEFORE HER CLASSES, THE BELLY EXPOSED
MONIKA CAN BE SEEN ON THE STREETS OF
BHAGSUNAG ANNOUNCING THE START OF
THE NEXT SESSION. WONDER IF GUYS CAN
SIGN UP TOO?

AVITAL PROMISES RECOVERY FROM ADDICTION, BUT WHY WOULD PEOPLE BUY THAT? AFTER ALL, THEY COME FROM ALL OVER THE WORLD TO DHARAMSALA TO GET ADDICTED ON THE CHEAP. SHE SEEMS TO BE SELLING COMBS IN THE LAND OF THE BALD.

MEDITATE AND REACH
'CLOUD NINE' OR GO
TO 'CLOUD NINE' TO
MEDITATE?

Shiva Dhaam.
UNIVERS
YOGA
Meditation
School
Contact at,
Cloud Nine
with OM
Morning Class
9:00 TO
11:00 AM

BUDDHA HALL
OPP. GERMAN BAKERY BHAGSUNAG PH: 221171

LEARN REIKI
. HOW DOES REIKI WORKS.
. SELF HEALING.
. KNOW ABOUT SEVEN MAIN ENERGY CENTERS
. EXPERIENCE OF CHANNELLING IN REIKI   MORE
DETAILS CONTACT. Mrs. USHA-REIKI MASTER AT BUDHA HALL.

CENTER FOR YOGA
MEDITATION . REIKI MUSIC DANCE
& OTHER CULTURAL ACTIVITIES.
HALL FOR RENT 4 ANY KIND OF
ACTIVITIES
यहाँ पर पोस्टर लगाना सख्त मना है ।

Enjoy **CONCERT OF**
INDIAN CLASSICAL MUSIC BY
FAMOUS MUSICIAN:LEARNING FACILITIES
ALSO AVAILABLE .SITAR .FLUTE.TABLA
SHANAI . VOCAL . SAROD

OF all
G'S

TATTOO
SHOP

GO TO THE BUDDHA HALL TO ATTEND ANY OF
THESE COURSES. AND WHEN THEY HAVE NO
TAKERS, YOU CAN RENT THE HALL AND DO YOUR
OWN 'ACTIVITIES' THERE

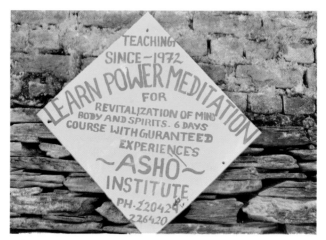

THE MIND AND BODY ARE FINE, BUT DO YOU
WANT TO INVOKE THE 'SPIRITS' BY
'REVITALIZING' THEM?

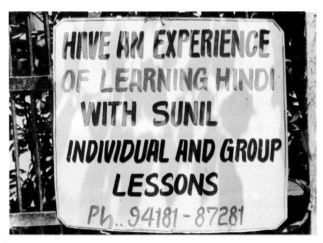

I SPENT HALF MY LIFE AND MY DAD'S SAVINGS IN A
SCHOOL, AND NO ONE TOLD ME THERE WAS A
CRASH COURSE OPTION AVAILABLE!!

SOMEONE NEEDS TO CHECK THE APOSTROPHES

THE MASTERS PROMISE TO DO WONDERS WITH
YOU IN AN HOUR

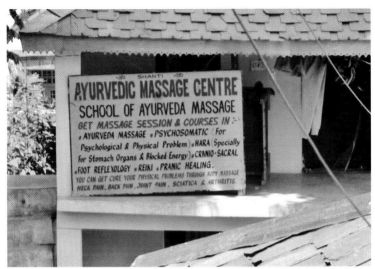

WHY GO TO MEDICAL SCHOOL FOR YEARS WHEN YOU CAN BECOME A DOCTOR HERE IN DAYS?

CHECK OUT THE CHEERFUL SOUNDING EMAIL ADDRESS AT THE BOTTOM

In Bhagsunag near Mcleodganj <<
in Himachal Pradesh

DO THESE 'AD' UP?

These are sights one should capture on their 'steal' - oops, I mean still - and 'video movi' - more oops - cameras. Signboards and advertisements by local businesses may not always attract customers, but they sure do leave you smiling.

There is someone who promises 'tension free' shopping by being a 'No Discount Shop' - hence no bargaining. You are welcomed to 'Marry Land;' no idea what this shop meant, but the reference could be to Manali being a popular honeymoon destination where this shop is located. A Ladakhi and Kashmiri art shop in Leh calls itself 'Same Same But Different;' now that's one way to stand out from the competition.

And if the shopping has tired you out, go in for some 'power meditation' that promises a 'way for renovation of your body, mind and spirits.' (I thought one only renovated houses!!) Or some herbal massage for different parts of the body including the 'neek.' Don't miss the 'Foot Golden Silver' massage though.

And when you are done, hop on to a three-wheeled auto rickshaw in Manali for some 'local site seen.' We are sure it will all 'ad'd up to a great experience.

YOU KNOW YOU CANNOT
BARGAIN HERE, SO WHY WORRY?

MARRIAGES ARE MADE IN HEAVEN. HIMACHAL
PRADESH IS REGARDED THE LAND OF THE GODS.
WELCOME TO 'MARRY LAND!!'

Shopfronts in Manali in the <<
state of Himachal Pradesh

A three-wheeled auto <<
rickshaw in Manali

THIS IS A SIGHT IN ITSELF

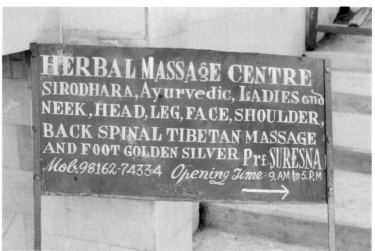

CAN YOU FIGURE OUT WHERE THE MASSAGE
STARTS AND WHERE IT ENDS?

WHERE DO MEN
GO TO RELAX?

In Bhagsunag near Mcleodganj in <<
Himachal Pradesh

Along the Manali - Rohtang Pass road where vendors <<
rent out suitable gear for those visiting the cold glacial
conditions at the Rohtang Pass

HOPE THE EQUIPMENT ON HIRE IS MORE RELIABLE THAN THE WAY THEY ARE SPELT!!

DIVERSITY IS
NOT JUST GOOD
POLITICS, IT IS
ALSO GOOD
MARKETING

IS HARD ROCK
CAFÉ FLATTERED
WITH THIS
IMITATION?

In Leh town in Ladakh <<

SAY HELLO TO
JOSHI WHEN
YOU GO THERE
Hindi Translation: Joshi
Hello Centre

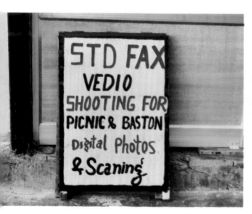

WHAT KIND OF
A PICNIC IS
'BASTON?'

Signs outside Public Call Office (PCO) where you can <<
make calls in Abbot Mount (Uttarakhand) and Padum
(Zanskar Valley, Ladakh) respectively

In Jispa, a town in Himachal <<
Pradesh en-route to Ladakh

WHEN DOES AN
'EX-SERVICEMAN'
BECOME AN
'EX-MAN?' WHEN
HE STARTS
SELLING
'KARYANA'
(GROCERIES)?

INTERESTING
NAME FOR A
COMPANY
PROVIDING
SECURITY
SERVICES

In a market in South Delhi <<

GETTING
HOSPITABLE

Just when you thought you had heard all about the cuisines of India, along comes a shack serving 'Good Happy Times' even as another café serves food with 'positive vibration.' You cannot be in India and ever have a drab meal; it is always peppered with surprises you least expect. And at the unlikeliest of places.

You could be in Tabo at the 'Third Eye Café' named after the Hindu God Shiva with three eyes and get to eat 'Indian, Chinese, Italian, Israeli and Continental Food.' It is also the place where the 'world meets.' Head to Mcleodganj where the Om Café will serve you 'Love' and offer rooms to stay; the Soul Food Café serves 'thick and chunky soups' besides many other items in its menu called 'Food for Life.'

If you are looking for even more out-of-the-world experiences, there are the Shangrila Café and the 'Laffing Budha Food Corner and Fresh Bakrey.' If dhabas, or streetside restaurants are what whet your appetite, the likes of Café Kathmandu on the way to Ladakh will serve you 'Ind and Chi dishes' while the Hozer Café on the same route will cook some 'Meggi' - Nestle's instant 'Maggi 2-minute' noodles - for you.

Take care when having any ice-cream in Manali though; the 'Black Current' flavour might just shock you.

In Bilaspur, a town on the way to <<
Manali from Delhi.

AND HURRY UP BEFORE THE TORTOISE
BEATS YOU TO IT

BACKPACKERS
COULD DO WITH
A 'SHAWER.'
ANYONE GOT A
WASHING
MACHINE TOO?

In Bhagsunag near Mcleodganj <<
in Himachal Pradesh

THE TEA ESTATE WAS 'REJUVENATED' SO THE TEA COULD 'REVIVE' YOU

Taken in and around Vijaypur, a <<
village in east Uttarakhand

IF YOU SEE THE CONDITION THIS SHOP IS IN,
YOU WILL NOT FEEL LIKE HAVING THE 'SPECIAL'

THIS DAILY
PROTEIN CENTRE
(WRITTEN IN
HINDI) SURE IS
NOT HEALTHY
FOR THE ANIMALS
DEPICTED

A shop in Champawat in east <<
Uttarakhand

IF YOU MISS THE 'REAL CAFFEINE' IN THESE PARTS, STOCK UP NOW

WITH SUCH A RANGE OF CUISINES, THE WORLD IS ALREADY PRESENT THERE

Taken in the town of Tabo in the Lahaul <<
Spiti region of Himachal Pradesh

IS THE BUDDHA
LAUGHING SEEING
THIS ONE?

In and around Mcleodganj in <<
Himachal Pradesh

WHAT WILL THE
SOUL DO WITH
SO MUCH FOOD?

IS IT 'QUITE A
PEACE' OR
'PEACE AND
QUIET?'

In Dharamkot near Mcleodganj in <<
Himachal Pradesh

FOUR SEASONS HAS COMPETITION: ROOMS, GLOBAL CUISINES AND LOVE ARE ON OFFER HERE

WELCOME TO UTOPIA

In Bhagsunag near Mcleodganj in <<
Himachal Pradesh

BE CAREFUL OF 'BLACK
CURRENTS;' THIS ICE
CREAM MAY SHOCK YOU

In Manali in <<
Himachal Pradesh

DO THEY MEAN KEEP PRESSING 'REFRESH'
WHEN BROWSING?

MAYBE YOU CAN
DOWNLOAD SOME
PEACE HERE

In Manali in <<
Himachal Pradesh

In Munsiyari in Uttarakhand <<

THE SPELLING WASN'T THE ONLY THING WRONG WITH THIS RESORT…

…BUT THE FOOD HERE WAS AS GOOD AS THE INVITING SIGN OUTSIDE

In Vijaypur in east <<
Uttarakhand

HERE COMES THE SUN. TO HEAT WATER.

A signpost for a resort in <<
Musiyari in Uttarakhand

WE KEPT LOOKING FOR CAVES 'AMIDST' THE RESORT

In Patal Bhuwaneswar in <<
Uttarakhand, location of
some ancient underground
caves of religious
significance for the Hindus

DO THEY HAVE 'CATTOGES' TOO?

Signpost for a camp <<
in Munsiyari

THAT'S MORE COMPETITION FOR FOUR SEASONS:
YOU GET A BED FOR A DOLLAR A NIGHT HERE

IF YOU WANT TO BE AUDIBLE ON THE BUSY
HIGHWAY WHERE THIS SHACK IS LOCATED, DON'T
'WISHPER' - OOPS, WHISPER

Dhabas, or highway eating shacks, on <<
the Manali - Ladakh route

ONE REALLY FEELS 'GOOD, HAPPY TIMES'
ARE BACK HERE

At a shack in Triund, a three-hour trek <<
away from Mcleodganj in Himachal
Pradesh

THESE KIOSKS SHOULD HAVE BEEN AT THE BEIJING OLYMPICS

Spotted on the route from <<
Manali to Ladakh

MAY WE ALSO 'STEP IN?'

Between Rohtang Pass and <<
Jispa in Himachal Pradesh

DOES THIS PUNJABI
DHABA, OR ROADSIDE
CAFÉ, ALSO HAVE FOOD
ON ITS MENU?

Near Dharamsala in <<
Himachal Pradesh

MONASTY
ENTRY TICKET
FROM HERE

At the entrance of the Hemis Monastery <<
near Leh in Ladakh

NOTICED IN
PUBLIC
INTEREST

You have to hand it to the creativity of those who put up notices for the general public. There is a polite sign at the Thiksey Monastery in Ladakh which asks you to 'take off your shoes my dear friends' in the library. A garbage basket also beckons passers-by in Manali to 'give me the garbage' in Hindi.

Or you have the Mayavati Ashram where they ask you to 'commit nuisance' only in the 'latrines' (toilets) and nowhere else in the hospital. If you want to save yourself any 'shocking experiences' it is important to 'practice proper electricity safety,' according to the Delhi Metro Rail Corporation. And if any travel service providers in Ladakh falls short, the authorities could be asked to cancel his registration as well as subject him to 'milder measures.'

If you fail to pay heed to public messages, you could be 'prohibited' from other travels: No, this is not my word; the Archaeological Survey of India has marked an area as 'prohibited' in Patal Bhuvaneshwar in Uttarakhand. I think they meant 'protected' but one never knows with these departments, right?

ATTENTION PLEASE.

1. PHOTOGRAPHY IS STRICKLY PROHIBITED IN-SIDE THE TEMPLES.
2. SMOKING & CONSUMING ALCOHOLIK DRINKS IN THE VICINITY OF THE TEMPLES ALSO STRICKLY PROHIBITED.
3. PLEASE COOPERATE WITH THE MANAGEMENT TO KEEP THE ENVIRONMENT OF THE TEMPLES NEAT AND CLEAN.

MANAGEMENT
(LIKIR MONASTARY)
LEH

VIDEOGRAPHY IN THE MUSEUM IS STRICKLY PROHIBITED. PLEASE DEPOSIT ALL VIDEO CAMERA & OTHER PHOTO-GRAPIC GADGMETS INCLUDING MOBILE PHONE HERE.
(MANAGEMENT COMMITTEE)

IS A WORD PROCESSOR WITH SPELL CHECK ALLOWED?

Notices at the Alchi Monastery <<
and the Hemis Monastery in
Ladakh respectively

At the entrance to the library <<
of the Thiksey Monastery near
Leh in Ladakh

THIS IS WHAT POLITENESS IS ALL ABOUT

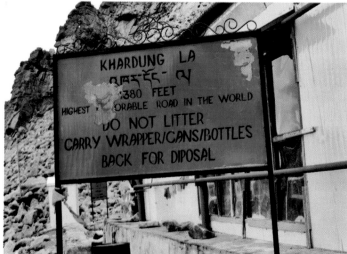

NOT A BLADE OF GRASS TO BE FOUND HERE,
BUT GREEN CONCERNS ARE NO LESS HERE

At the Khardung La (Pass) on the way <<
from Leh to Nubra Valley in Ladakh

At the Mayavati Ashram near <<
Champawat in eastern Uttarakhand

MAKE SURE YOU MAKE A 'NUISANCE' OF YOURSELF ONLY IN THE TOILETS (THE WORD 'LATRINES' IN POINT 2 MEANS TOILETS)

DEAR VISITOR

TRAVEL AGENTS ASSOCIATION OF LADAKH (TAAL)
WELCOMES YOU TO LADAKH.
AN ASSOCIATION OF ALL THE REGISTERED TRAVEL AGENTS TO
SAFEGUARD THEIR INTEREST AND TO PROVIDE
BETTER SERVICE TO VISITERS.
- IN CASE A TRAVEL AGENTS DOES NOT PROVIDE THE PROMISED SERVICES OR
MISBEHAVES IN ANY OTHER WAY PLEASE CONTACT TAAL, THE ERRANT-
TRAVEL AGENT RISK BEING BLACKLISTED AND A RECOMMENDATION TO THE-
AUTHORITIES TO CANCEL HIS REGISTRATION APART FROM THE MILDER-
MEASURE.
- USING THE SERVICES OF A REGISTERED TRAVEL AGENT WILL MAKE THE RESCUE
OPERATIONS QUICKER AND EASIER IN CASE OF AN ACCIDENT ON A TREK.
- GLACIAL STREAMS ARE THE LIFE LINE OF LADAKHI VILLAGES -PLEASE STRICTLY
INSTRUCTOR YOUR STAFF TO MAINTAIN THEIR SANCTITY WHILE ON A TREK.
WISH YOU A NICE VISIT/STAY

WONDER WHAT MILDER MEASURES WOULD
BE TAKEN?

Notice in Leh town <<
in Ladakh

THIS SHOCKING BUSINESS SEEMS TO BE ALL
OVER THE PLACE

Banner put up the construction site <<
of the Delhi Metro Rail

SOMEONE SHOULD
'PROHIBIT' PEOPLE
WRITING SUCH SIGNS

Notice at the site of the ancient Hindu <<
religious caves in Patal Bhuwaneshwar
in eastern Uttarakhand
managed by ASI (Archaeological
Survey of India)

In Leh town. Polythin refers <<
to Polythene or Plastic.

In Manali. The sign translates <<
to 'Give me the garbage.'

GREEN AND CLEAN: THE MANTRA WE ALL
NEED TO CHANT

THE END

WOULD HAVE TURNED AROUND FOR A BOW BUT
TOO MANY SIGNS TO GO